COOKING HAS NEVER BEEN **THIS EASY!**

Goof proof
COOKING

Goof Proof? Absolutely!

With these simple recipes, you can make foods that are both impressive and delicious. Step-by-step directions show you how to combine a handful of flavorful ingredients into a memorable meal without fail. Perfect for beginners and experienced cooks who want easy preps with great results.

Abbreviations & Cheats

T. = tablespoon

tsp. = teaspoon

C. = cup

1 T. = 3 teaspoons

¼ C. = 4 tablespoons

1 stick of butter = ½ cup = 8 tablespoons

ISBN-13: 978-1-56383-624-4
Item #7150

Printed in the USA by G&R Publishing Co.

Distributed By:

507 Industrial Street
Waverly, IA 50677

www.cqbookstore.com

gifts@cqbookstore.com

 CQ Products

 CQ Products

 @cqproducts

 @cqproducts

MEASURE IT RIGHT...

1. **Liquids-** Set a clear, spouted cup like this on the counter and check the markings at eye level.

2. **Dry ingredients, small pieces, and soft solids *(like sour cream)*-** Spoon the food into graduated cups like these and level off with the straight edge of a knife or spatula to get rid of the extra. Brown sugar? Pack it firmly into the cup or measuring spoon.

3. **Small amounts-** Fill the correct measuring spoon to the top with dry or liquid ingredients.

How Do I...

Peel and dice an onion

Slice off both ends and peel off the papery covering. Slice partway through the onion "rings" in both directions in a grid pattern, then turn the onion on its side and thinly slice to get small pieces.

Drain foods

Set a colander or wire mesh strainer over a bowl or measuring cup. Add food and let the liquid drain off into the bowl. Discard the liquid if it's not needed, or reserve the amount required for the recipe.

Break and separate an egg

Crack an egg on the edge of a bowl (or on the counter) and pull the halves apart with your thumbs. To separate the yolk and white, slip the yolk back and forth between eggshell halves, letting the white drop into a bowl. Dig out stray shell pieces with an eggshell half.

Simmer and boil foods

To **simmer**, cook food gently in liquid so small bubbles form and begin to break the surface. To **boil**, increase heat until the liquid gets hotter and big bubbles break through the surface constantly. Cover with a lid to make this process quicker.

Handle a hard-cooked egg

After hard-cooked eggs are cold, crack the shell on the countertop and gently peel it off. Use an egg slicer for thin, even slices or chop the egg with a sharp knife.

Test food for doneness

Test a baked omelet by sliding a knife into the center – if it comes out clean, your egg dish is done. Poke cooked vegetables with a fork: a fork will go through "tender" veggies easily; "crisp-tender" ones are still a little firm. Test center of meat with an instant-read thermometer.

Grilled Honey-Dijon Chicken

✔ ¼ to ⅓ C. Dijon mustard
✔ 3 T. honey
✔ 3 T. snipped fresh parsley

✔ 4 boneless, skinless chicken breast halves
✔ Salt and black pepper, optional

1 Preheat your grill to medium heat and brush the grill grate with olive oil.

2 In a small bowl, stir together mustard, honey, and parsley; set sauce aside.

3 Place chicken pieces between two pieces of waxed paper or plastic wrap and flatten each piece with the flat side of a meat mallet to an even thickness, about ½".

4 Set chicken on the grill grate and cook about 3 minutes. Flip chicken and brush generously with set-aside mustard sauce. Grill 2 to 3 minutes more or until golden brown, juices just run clear, and internal temperature reaches 165° with an instant-read meat thermometer. Transfer chicken to a platter and cover loosely with foil; let stand about 5 minutes. Season with salt and pepper if you'd like.

Add flavor with herbs

Fresh and dried herbs can be used interchangeably in recipes, but use three times more of the fresh stuff because dry herbs have a more concentrated flavor. (For example, in this recipe, you would need just 1 T. dry parsley flakes.)

KITCHEN SHEARS

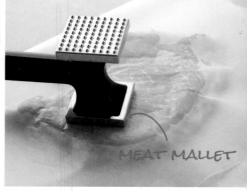

MEAT MALLET

BASTING BRUSH

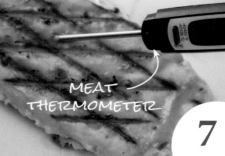

MEAT
THERMOMETER

PARMESAN-PEPPER
BREADSTICKS P. 61

Creamy Potato Soup
WITH PARMESAN-PEPPER BREADSTICKS

- ✔ 3 to 4 large baking potatoes
- ✔ ½ onion
- ✔ 1 (32 oz.) container chicken broth
- ✔ 1 (8 oz.) pkg. cream cheese, cubed
- ✔ 1 tsp. ground marjoram
- ✔ Seasoned salt, black pepper, and/or cayenne pepper, optional

1 Wash and peel the potatoes. Cut them into cubes *(you'll need about 4 cups cubed potatoes)*. Peel and dice enough onion to measure ⅓ cup. Put both vegetables into a large saucepan or medium soup pot.

2 Pour the broth over vegetables and give it a stir. Cover and bring to a boil over medium heat. Reduce heat to medium-low and cook until potatoes are fork tender, about 20 minutes.

3 With a potato masher, smash some of the potatoes to thicken the soup. Stir in the marjoram.

4 Reduce heat to low. Add cream cheese and continue to cook, stirring often, until cheese melts and soup is hot. Stir in seasoned salt, black pepper, and/or cayenne pepper if you'd like.

VEGETABLE PEELER

POTATO MASHER

9

ZIPPY GLAZED
CARROTS P. 63

Chicken Cordon Bleu
WITH ZIPPY GLAZED CARROTS

- ✔ 2 boneless, skinless chicken breast halves
- ✔ 4 slices deli-style ham
- ✔ 2 slices Swiss cheese
- ✔ ½ C. seasoned bread crumbs

1 Preheat the oven to 350°. Coat an 8 x 8" baking dish with cooking spray.

2 Place the chicken between layers of plastic wrap or waxed paper and use the flat side of a meat mallet to pound each piece to about ¼" thickness. Place two slices of ham and a slice of cheese on top of each flattened chicken breast and roll them up into two tidy bundles, tucking in the ends to hold the fillings inside. Secure with toothpicks.

3 Spread the bread crumbs on a plate and coat each chicken bundle in crumbs. Set bundles in the baking dish and bake for 30 to 40 minutes or until no longer pink inside *(165°)*. For added browning, spritz with cooking spray and set under the broiler for a minute or two.

Buyer Alert!

If you ask for "a boneless, skinless chicken breast" at the meat counter, you might get a whole breast, which is actually two breast pieces connected by a thin membrane in the middle. Slice through the membrane and you'll get two "chicken breast halves." Some stores trim the breasts further into thin cutlets, which cook very quickly.

Chippy Popcorn Chicken
WITH Apple Coleslaw

- ✔ 2¼ lbs. boneless, skinless chicken breasts
- ✔ 1 (8 oz.) bag plain or flavored potato chips
- ✔ ½ C. butter
- ✔ 2 tsp. minced garlic
- ✔ Your favorite dipping sauce

1 Preheat the oven to 475° Cover a large rimmed baking sheet with foil and coat it with cooking spray.

2 Cut the chicken into 1" pieces, trimming off any excess fat.

3 Put the potato chips in a large zippered plastic bag, zip it closed, and crush the chips well with a rolling pin. Pour the crumbs onto a large plate and set aside.

4 In a small saucepan over low heat, melt the butter. Remove from heat and stir in the garlic; let it cool slightly.

5 Dip each chicken piece into the garlic butter and roll in crumbs until well coated. Arrange pieces on the baking sheet and bake 10 to 12 minutes or until crust is light golden brown and chicken is no longer pink inside *(165° with an instant-read thermometer)*. Serve with dipping sauce.

Try this...

Maple-Dijon Dipping Sauce
In a bowl, stir together ¼ C. real maple syrup, ¼ C. plain Greek yogurt, 2 T. Dijon mustard, and a dash of black pepper. Refrigerate until serving.

SERVES 4-6

APPLE COLESLAW
P. 61

ROLLING PIN

TONGS

13

Monte Cristo Egg Bake

- ✔ 4 eggs
- ✔ 1½ C. milk
- ✔ Salt and black pepper to taste
- ✔ 6 C. cubed ciabatta or French bread
- ✔ 1 (7.5 oz.) pkg. chopped ham (about 1½ C.)
- ✔ 1½ C. shredded Swiss cheese, divided
- ✔ Strawberry or raspberry preserves, optional

1 Preheat the oven to 350°. Coat a 9 x 9" baking dish with cooking spray.

2 Mix the eggs, milk, salt, and pepper in a big bowl, whisking well. Add the bread and stir until evenly coated. Stir in the ham and half the cheese.

3 Spoon the mixture into the dish and sprinkle with remaining cheese. Bake 40 minutes or until set and golden brown. Serve with some preserves if you'd like.

Pork Chops & French Rice

- 2 (10.5 oz.) cans French onion soup
- 1 C. uncooked long grain white rice
- 4 bone-in pork chops (½˝ to ¾˝ thick)
- Pork seasoning or seasoned salt
- 2 to 3 T. vegetable oil

1 Preheat the oven to 375°. Coat a 9 x 13" baking dish with cooking spray. Mix the soup and rice together in the dish and spread evenly.

2 Sprinkle both sides of pork chops with pork seasoning. Heat oil in a large skillet over medium-high heat. When hot, add the chops and brown them quickly on both sides.

3 Remove chops from the skillet and set them on top of rice mixture in baking dish. Cover tightly with foil and bake 40 minutes or until rice is tender. *(Be careful when removing foil as the escaping steam can burn.)*

SERVES 4-6

16

Simple Turkey Pot Pie

- ✔ 1 (14.1 oz.) pkg. refrigerated pie crusts (2 crusts)
- ✔ 1¾ C. frozen mixed vegetables or peas & carrots
- ✔ 2 C. shredded cooked turkey or chicken (use leftovers or rotisserie chicken)
- ✔ 1 (10.7 oz.) can cream of chicken soup
- ✔ Seasoned salt and black pepper to taste

1 Let crusts soften at room temperature for 15 minutes. Preheat the oven to 400°. Put the vegetables in a colander and rinse with warm water to partially thaw; drain well.

2 In a medium bowl, stir together the turkey, vegetables, and soup. Stir in seasoned salt and pepper as desired and set aside.

3 Unroll one crust and press it into an ungreased 9" pie plate *(crust edge may hang over the plate but that's alright)*. Spoon the turkey mixture into the crust and dampen the edge of the crust with water. Unroll the remaining crust and place it on top, pressing lightly around rim.

4 Trim off the extra crust with a knife and seal the crusts together with a fork. Cut slits or vents in the top crust with a sharp knife and spritz with cooking spray to increase browning. Bake 40 to 50 minutes or until crust is golden brown.

Don't throw away the crust trimmings...

Turn them into something sweet! Spritz leftover crust pieces with cooking spray and sprinkle with cinnamon and sugar. Bake 15 or 20 minutes or until golden brown and crisp.

Kickin' Beef Enchilada Bake

- ✔ 1 lb. lean ground beef
- ✔ 1 (16 oz.) jar black bean & corn salsa
- ✔ 1 (10 oz.) can mild enchilada sauce, divided
- ✔ 1 (8 oz.) pkg. shredded Mexican cheese (2 C.), divided
- ✔ 10 (6") corn tortillas or 8 (8") flour tortillas
- ✔ Optional toppings (sour cream, diced tomatoes, and/or avocado)

1. Preheat the oven to 350°. Coat a 9 x 13" baking dish with cooking spray and set it aside.

2. In a large skillet over medium heat, cook the beef until no longer pink, crumbling it with a wooden spoon as it cooks; drain. Stir in the salsa, ¼ cup enchilada sauce, and 1 cup of the cheese.

3. Wrap the stack of tortillas in paper towels and microwave for 45 seconds. Dividing the beef mixture evenly among tortillas, spoon some down the center of each one and roll up. Place tortillas seam side down in the baking dish.

4. Pour the remaining enchilada sauce over the top and sprinkle with the remaining 1 cup cheese. Cover with sprayed foil and bake 40 to 45 minutes or until hot and bubbly. Serve with your favorite toppings.

Cheese on the cheap

To save money, buy blocks of cheese and shred it yourself. Double-wrap the remaining block in foil or plastic wrap to prolong its freshness in the refrigerator. Bags of already-shredded cheese are usually more expensive but very convenient.

BAKED POTATO
P. 62

ROASTED BRUSSELS
SPROUTS P. 61

Lazy BBQ Ribs
WITH ROASTED BRUSSELS SPROUTS & BAKED POTATO

- ✔ 2 to 2½ lbs. baby back pork ribs
- ✔ ⅓ C. dark brown sugar
- ✔ 2½ T. Cajun seasoning
- ✔ Your favorite barbecue sauce

1 Preheat the oven to 300°. Cut the ribs into two equal sections, if necessary. Cut a piece of heavy-duty foil large enough so it will wrap around the ribs generously. Set the foil on a rimmed baking sheet and top with a piece of parchment paper. Set the ribs on the paper.

2 In a small bowl, mix the brown sugar and seasoning. Sprinkle the mixture over ribs and rub it in with your hands to generously coat all sides. Wrap the foil and parchment paper around the ribs and seal well. Place baking sheet and foil pack in the oven to bake for 3 hours or until tender.

3 Remove from oven, open the pack to expose ribs, and spread with barbecue sauce. Return to the oven and bake 20 to 30 minutes more. Meat should pull away from the bones when done. Cut into serving portions as needed.

21

Easiest Ravioli Lasagna

- ✔ 1 lb. lean ground beef, pork, or turkey
- ✔ 1 (24 oz.) jar spaghetti sauce
- ✔ 1 (20 oz.) pkg. frozen beef, sausage, or cheese ravioli
- ✔ 1½ C. shredded mozzarella cheese
- ✔ ¼ C. shredded Parmesan cheese, optional

1 Preheat the oven to 400°. Coat a 9 x 13" baking dish with cooking spray and set it aside.

2 In a large skillet over medium heat, cook the beef until no longer pink, crumbling it with a wooden spoon as it cooks; drain the meat.

3 Spread ⅓ of the spaghetti sauce over the bottom of the baking dish. Layer half each of the ravioli and cooked beef over sauce and sprinkle ½ cup mozzarella cheese on top. Repeat the layers of sauce, ravioli, beef, and mozzarella. Top with remaining sauce, mozzarella, and optional Parmesan cheese.

4 Cover with sprayed foil and bake about 40 minutes or until heated through. Let stand 10 minutes before serving.

Drain it easily

*Buying lean ground beef means there's less grease after it's browned. But it's still a good idea to drain the cooked meat before combining it with other ingredients. Just transfer the meat from the skillet to a **colander** or **wire mesh strainer** set over a bowl and let any grease drain off. When cool, discard the grease.*

Chicken Strip Pizza Boats

- ✔ 5 to 6 frozen breaded chicken strips, thawed*
- ✔ 1 (16 oz.) pkg. frozen garlic bread loaf, sliced lengthwise
- ✔ ¾ C. pizza sauce
- ✔ 1½ C. shredded Italian cheese blend
- ✔ Fresh parsley or oregano, optional

1 Preheat the oven to 400°. Cut thawed chicken strips into ½" pieces.

2 Arrange the garlic bread halves on a rimmed baking sheet, buttered side up. Bake for 8 to 9 minutes or until bread just begins to brown.

3 Remove from oven and spread pizza sauce over the top. Cover the sauce with chicken pieces and sprinkle the cheese on top. Bake 8 to 10 minutes more or until hot and melty. Sprinkle with fresh herbs before serving.

* These chicken strips are already cooked. Thaw them in the refrigerator overnight.

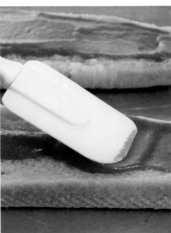

SERVES 4

ZESTY ORANGE
SAUCE

Crispy Coconut Shrimp
WITH ZESTY ORANGE SAUCE

- ✔ 1 (12 oz.) pkg. frozen large raw shrimp, deveined
- ✔ ¼ C. cornstarch
- ✔ 1½ C. sweetened flaked coconut
- ✔ 2 egg whites
- ✔ Cocktail sauce, optional

1 Thaw shrimp according to package directions. Peel off the shells, but leave the tails unpeeled. Rinse and pat dry with paper towels. Preheat the oven to 400°. Lightly coat a rimmed baking sheet with cooking spray and set everything aside.

2 Place the cornstarch, coconut, and egg whites in separate bowls. Whisk the egg whites until they're good and foamy.

3 Working with one shrimp at a time, lightly coat it in cornstarch. Then dip it into the egg white and roll it in coconut until evenly coated. Place shrimp on the baking sheet and repeat with remaining shrimp.

4 Bake for 15 to 20 minutes, flipping them halfway through cooking time, until shrimp are pink and coconut is browned. Serve with your favorite cocktail sauce or try the recipe below for dipping yumminess.

Zesty Orange Sauce

In a bowl, stir together ½ C. orange marmalade, 1 T. creamy horseradish, 1 T. Dijon mustard, and a dash of salt until well mixed. Refrigerate until serving.

Fiesta Sloppy Joes

- ✔ 1 ¼ lbs. lean ground beef
- ✔ ½ C. diced onion
- ✔ 1 (10.75 oz.) can fiesta nacho cheese soup
- ✔ ⅓ C. ketchup
- ✔ 6 hamburger buns

1 In a large skillet over medium-high heat, cook the ground beef and onion together until meat is brown and onion is tender, crumbling the meat with a wooden spoon as it cooks. Drain off the grease.

2 Add the soup and ketchup to the meat in skillet, stirring to blend. Cover and cook on low for 15 minutes or until heated through, stirring occasionally. Serve on buns.

Chicken Taco Soup

- ✔ 1 T. canola oil
- ✔ 1 C. diced onion
- ✔ 1 (12 to 13 oz.) pkg. frozen Southwest-style vegetables (we used the protein blend with seasoning)
- ✔ 1 (14.5 oz.) can diced tomatoes
- ✔ 1 (32 oz.) carton chicken broth

- ✔ Taco seasoning to taste
- ✔ 1 (1 oz.) packet taco seasoning
- ✔ 2 C. shredded cooked chicken (use leftovers or rotisserie chicken)
- ✔ Optional toppings (shredded cheddar cheese, tortilla chips, and/or guacamole)

1 Heat oil in a medium soup pot over medium heat. Add the onion and cook until softened. Stir in the vegetables and cook 1 to 2 minutes more, stirring frequently.

2 Add the tomatoes *(with juice)*, broth, taco seasoning, and chicken; stir to combine and bring to a boil.

3 Reduce heat to low and simmer 15 minutes longer, stirring occasionally. Sprinkle with toppings before serving.

29

BLT Pasta Salad

- ✔ *8 oz. uncooked small shell pasta*
- ✔ *½ lb. bacon strips*
- ✔ *¾ C. ranch dressing*
- ✔ *½ C. chopped red onion*
- ✔ *2 tomatoes, diced, divided*
- ✔ *Salad greens*

1 Bring a big pot of lightly salted water to a boil. Add the pasta and cook according to package directions until al dente or slightly softer, but do not overcook. Drain pasta in a colander and rinse well under cold water.

2 In a big skillet over medium-high heat, cook the bacon until browned and crisp; drain on paper towels and discard grease. When cool, crumble the bacon and set aside.

3 In a large bowl, combine the dressing, onion, and half the tomato. Add the cooled pasta, stirring until well coated. Cover and refrigerate several hours *(or overnight)*.

4 To serve, spoon pasta salad onto greens and top with set-aside bacon and remaining tomato.

Pasta, Pasta, Pasta

*Cooking your pasta to "**al dente**" means it will be tender, but still firm enough to hold its shape well. Check the doneness by cutting with a fork; it should give a slight resistance when cut or chewed. Nearly any shape will work for this recipe.*

Puffy Pizza Bake

- ✔ 2 (7.5 oz.) pouches Bisquick Complete Buttermilk Biscuit Mix
- ✔ 1 C. water
- ✔ 1 (15 oz.) bottle pizza sauce, divided
- ✔ 1 (7 to 8 oz.) pkg. sliced pepperoni, divided
- ✔ 1 (8 oz.) pkg. shredded mozzarella cheese (2 C.), divided

1 Preheat the oven to 375°. Coat a 9 x 13" baking dish with cooking spray and set it aside.

2 Empty both pouches of biscuit mix into a medium bowl and add water; stir together until a soft dough forms. Drop half of the dough by the spoonful evenly over the bottom of baking dish *(dough will not cover it completely)*.

3 Drizzle about half the pizza sauce over the dough. Arrange half the pepperoni slices evenly over the sauce. Top with 1 cup cheese. Repeat the layers with remaining dough, sauce, pepperoni, and cheese.

4 Bake 20 to 25 minutes or until light golden brown. Cut into squares to serve.

Personalize

Personalize your pizza by adding other favorite ingredients like **mushrooms**, **onions**, **peppers**, **Canadian bacon**, **bacon**, **cheddar cheese**, **green** *or* **black olives**, *or* **anchovies**. *You may need to increase the baking time slightly. For a different crust, try pouches of* **3-cheese** *or* **cheese-garlic biscuit mix**.

Savory Apricot Chicken

- ✔ 4 boneless, skinless chicken breast halves
- ✔ 1 (10 oz.) jar apricot jam (about 1 C.)
- ✔ 1 C. Russian salad dressing
- ✔ 1 (1 oz.) packet dry onion soup mix
- ✔ Cooked rice, couscous, or noodles, optional

1 Preheat the oven to 350°. Arrange the chicken in an ungreased 9 x 13" baking dish and set it aside.

2 In a bowl, mix the jam, dressing, and soup mix until blended. Pour all of the mixture over the chicken.

3 Bake uncovered for 40 to 50 minutes, spooning some of the sauce over the chicken after 30 minutes of cooking. Chicken is done when a meat thermometer registers 165° and it's no longer pink inside. Serve chicken and sauce over cooked rice, couscous, or noodles if you'd like.

Try something different

Mix one of these sauces and pour it over the chicken breast halves in place of the apricot sauce above. Same chicken, same process, but different delicious flavors!

Sweet & Saucy Chicken: *Mix 1⅓ C. salsa, ¼ C. brown sugar, and 4 tsp. honey Dijon mustard. Bake as directed above.*

Coca-Cola Chicken: *Mix 1 (12 oz.) can Coke, ½ C. ketchup, and ¼ C. honey barbecue sauce. Cover this dish with foil and bake it 50 to 60 minutes.*

Chili-Glazed Smoked Chops
WITH SOUR CREAM POTATOES & ROASTED VEGGIES

- ✔ Juice from 1 orange (about 3 T.)
- ✔ 2 T. brown sugar
- ✔ 1 T. chili powder
- ✔ ½ tsp. garlic powder
- ✔ ½ tsp. dry mustard
- ✔ 6 smoked pork chops (1" thick)

1 Preheat the oven to 400°. Line a rimmed baking sheet with foil and spritz with cooking spray. Arrange pork chops in a single layer on the foil.

2 In a small bowl, whisk together orange juice, brown sugar, chili powder, garlic powder, and dry mustard. Brush the mixture over the chops.

3 Bake uncovered for 20 to 25 minutes or until chops are heated through (145°) and glaze is caramelized.

What is a smoked chop?

Most smoked pork chops from a meat case are fully cooked. You should still heat them to an internal temperature of 145° before eating, but they'll have a smoky, ham-like flavor that is different from regular pork chops, which are raw when you buy them and need to be fully cooked.

SERVES 8

SIMPLE POTATO SALAD
P. 62

38

Low & Slow Pulled Pork
WITH SIMPLE POTATO SALAD

- ✔ 2 onions
- ✔ 1 (4 lb.) pork roast, such as boneless shoulder roast
- ✔ Dry rub* or pork seasoning
- ✔ 1 C. ginger ale
- ✔ Hamburger buns

1 Preheat the oven to 275°. Peel and slice the onions; lay half the slices in a roasting pan or 9 x 13" baking pan.

2 If your roast comes wrapped in netting, leave it in place. Roll the roast in the dry rub to coat well and then pat it in place. Set the roast in the pan. Place remaining onion slices on and around meat.

3 Slowly pour the ginger ale over the roast and onions. Cover and bake about 4 hours or until meat is very tender and dark *(check after 3 hours)*. Uncover for the last 15 to 30 minutes of cooking time.

4 Remove the meat from pan, cut the netting, and pull it off the meat, if applicable. Shred the pork with two forks and return it to the pan with the juice and onions. Stir and keep warm.

5 Lift meat and onions out of the juice and serve on buns with condiments as desired.

What's the rub?

*A **dry rub** is a mixture of spices that is spread on meat before cooking to add flavor and color. To make your own rub, mix 4 tsp. seasoned salt, 1 tsp. sugar, ¼ tsp. black pepper, ⅛ tsp. each dry mustard and ground cumin, and a pinch each of ground ginger and cayenne pepper.*

Beef & Broccoli Stir-Fry

- ✔ 1¼ lbs. beef sirloin or flank steak
- ✔ 1 (1 oz.) packet stir-fry seasoning mix (such as Kikkoman brand)
- ✔ Water
- ✔ 1 large red bell pepper
- ✔ Peanut oil
- ✔ 2 C. small broccoli florets
- ✔ Cooked rice or noodles, optional

1 Slice the beef into thin 2"-long strips *(the thinner, the better)* and place them in a large zippered plastic bag. In a small bowl, stir together seasoning mix and 1 cup water; pour over the meat. Seal the bag and let meat marinate for 30 minutes to develop flavor.

2 Remove the stem and seeds from bell pepper and slice into thin strips.

3 Drain the beef in a colander set over a bowl and reserve the marinade. Heat 1 tablespoon oil in a large skillet over high heat. Add the meat; cook and stir until beef is no longer pink and begins to brown *(pour off excess liquid as needed)*. Transfer the meat to a clean bowl and carefully wipe out the skillet.

4 To the empty skillet, add 1 tablespoon oil. When hot, stir in the broccoli and cook over high heat for 2 minutes. Add bell pepper strips and cook for another minute, stirring frequently. Add 2 tablespoons water, cover the skillet quickly, and cook vegetables over medium-high heat 2 to 4 minutes more or until crisp-tender, stirring occasionally.

5 Return the beef and reserved marinade to the skillet; stir and cook 1 to 2 minutes until sauce thickens and food is coated. Serve over cooked rice or noodles if you'd like.

Curried Shrimp & Potatoes

- ✔ 12 to 16 oz. frozen large raw shrimp, deveined
- ✔ 2 large baking potatoes
- ✔ 2 or 3 green onions
- ✔ 3 T. vegetable oil
- ✔ 1½ to 2 tsp. curry powder
- ✔ Salt and black pepper to taste

1 Thaw shrimp according to package directions. Wash the potatoes and cut them into ½" cubes. Slice the white and light green parts of onions; reserve dark green parts. Peel shells off shrimp *(if intact)* and remove tails. Set everything aside.

2 In a large skillet, heat oil over medium-high heat. When hot, add potatoes, spreading them out. Cook without stirring for 5 to 6 minutes or until undersides are brown. Carefully flip potatoes and brown the other side about 5 minutes.

3 Toss in the sliced onions and cook 1 minute more. With a slotted spoon or spatula, transfer potatoes and onions to a paper towel-lined plate.

4 Add shrimp and curry powder to the skillet and cook for 2 to 3 minutes or until shrimp are pink, stirring occasionally. Return potatoes and onions to the skillet; cook and stir until heated through. Season with salt and pepper and cut reserved onion greens over the top.

Where to find it

Curry powder is a blend of spices usually associated with Indian cooking. You can find it in the spice aisle of your grocery store.

Bacon-Lover's Mac & Cheese

- ✔ 8 oz. uncooked elbow macaroni
- ✔ 3 C. shredded cheddar and/or Velveeta cheese
- ✔ ¼ C. butter
- ✔ ¼ C. flour
- ✔ Black pepper to taste
- ✔ 2 C. milk
- ✔ ¾ tsp. smoked paprika
- ✔ 3 bacon strips, cooked & crumbled (or ¼ C. bacon bits)

1 Preheat the oven to 325° and spritz an 8 x 8" baking dish with cooking spray. Cook the macaroni in a saucepan of lightly salted boiling water following package directions until al dente; drain. Return pasta to the pan and sprinkle with cheese; let stand.

2 Meanwhile, in another saucepan, melt the butter over medium heat. Whisk in flour and pepper and cook 2 to 3 minutes. Slowly whisk in the milk, cooking over low heat until slightly thickened, stirring constantly.

3 Pour hot cream sauce over cheese and pasta; let stand until nearly melted. Stir together and then dump pasta into the baking dish. Sprinkle with paprika and bacon. Bake 12 to 15 minutes.

Mexican Omelet

- ✔ ½ C. salsa, plus more for serving
- ✔ 1 (8 oz.) pkg. shredded Mexican cheese (2 C.)
- ✔ 6 eggs
- ✔ 1 C. sour cream, plus more for serving

1 Preheat the oven to 350°. Spread ½ cup salsa over the bottom of an ungreased 9" or 10" pie plate. Sprinkle the cheese on top.

2 In a medium bowl, whisk together the eggs and 1 cup sour cream until smooth. Pour the egg mixture over the cheese layer.

3 Bake about 40 minutes or until edges are lightly browned and a knife inserted in the center comes out clean. Serve with more salsa and sour cream.

Lemony Blackened Salmon
WITH MASHED SWEET POTATOES

- 2 T. fresh lemon juice
- 1 to 2 tsp. chopped fresh parsley or dill
- 2 T. butter, melted
- ½ tsp. garlic powder
- Salt and black pepper to taste
- 4 salmon fillets, skin on
- 2 T. olive oil

1 Preheat the oven to 350°. In a small bowl, whisk together the lemon juice, parsley, butter, garlic powder, salt, and pepper.

2 Brush butter mixture over salmon pieces, coating both sides; set aside on a plate.

3 Heat the oil in a large oven-safe skillet over medium-high heat. When oil begins to smoke, add the salmon, skin side up. Cook until seared and golden brown on one side, 1 to 2 minutes.

4 Flip salmon pieces over, skin side down, and transfer skillet to the oven. Bake 6 to 8 minutes or just until fish flakes easily with a fork.

Juicing a lemon

Roll the lemon back and forth on the counter a few times and then cut it in half crosswise. If you have a citrus juicer or reamer, press and twist the cut sides of the lemon against its ridges to collect the juice. If not, simply squeeze the lemon halves over a bowl and remove the seeds.

MASHED SWEET
POTATOES P. 63

CITRUS JUICER

BASTING BRUSH

One-Pan Chicken Parm

- ✔ 1 egg
- ✔ 1 T. water
- ✔ ¾ C. Italian seasoned bread crumbs
- ✔ 1½ lbs. boneless, skinless chicken cutlets or strips
- ✔ 3 T. olive oil
- ✔ 8 oz. mozzarella cheese (sliced or shredded), divided
- ✔ 1 (24 oz.) jar spaghetti sauce
- ✔ ¼ C. grated Parmesan cheese
- ✔ 8 oz. uncooked spaghetti

1 Preheat the oven to 350°. Mix the egg and water in a shallow bowl and place bread crumbs in another bowl.

2 Dip chicken pieces in egg mixture and then coat in bread crumbs.

3 Heat the oil in a large oven-safe skillet over medium-high heat. Cook chicken 2 to 3 minutes on each side, until golden brown.

4 Top chicken with half the mozzarella cheese and then spoon sauce over everything. Sprinkle with Parmesan cheese and add remaining mozzarella. Bake 25 minutes or until sauce is bubbly and chicken is cooked through (165°).

5 Meanwhile, cook the spaghetti in lightly salted boiling water following package directions; drain. Serve the chicken and sauce over the hot spaghetti.

Porcupine Meatballs
WITH EASY CHEESY HASHBROWNS

- ✔ 1 lb. lean ground beef
- ✔ 1 (6.8 oz.) box Beef Rice A Roni
- ✔ 1 egg
- ✔ 2¼ C. beef broth

1 Put the ground beef in a medium bowl. Add the rice-vermicelli mixture from the Rice A Roni box, but set the seasoning packet aside for later use. Add the egg and mix everything together with your hands until well combined.

2 Shape the mixture into 16 to 18 meatballs, about the size of golf balls. Place the meatballs in a large skillet and cook over medium-high heat until browned on all sides, turning with tongs several times during cooking. Reduce heat to medium-low.

3 Whisk together the broth and seasoning from set-aside packet; pour the mixture over browned meatballs and bring to a simmer. Cover and simmer over low heat for 35 to 40 minutes or until much of the liquid has been absorbed and meatballs are cooked through *(160°)*. Cook uncovered for the last 5 minutes.

Keep 'em round

*If you brown the meatballs in a nonstick skillet, it's easy to turn them with **tongs** because they won't stick to the pan. Then you'll have nice round meatballs – and clean-up will be a snap.*

EASY CHEESY
HASHBROWNS P. 63

Speedy Vegetable Beef Soup

- ✔ 2 (10 to 12 oz.) pkgs. frozen vegetable combos*
- ✔ 1 C. frozen Southern-style hash brown potatoes
- ✔ 2 (14 oz.) cans beef broth
- ✔ ½ tsp. each Italian seasoning and garlic powder
- ✔ 2 C. shredded cooked roast beef (refrigerated 15 oz. pkg. in au jus or leftovers)
- ✔ ½ to 1 C. coarsely chopped fresh spinach, optional
- ✔ Salt and black pepper to taste

1 Empty frozen vegetables and potatoes into a big microwave-safe bowl, cover lightly, and microwave on high for 5 minutes.

2 In a medium soup pot, combine the broth, Italian seasoning, and garlic powder. Bring to a boil over medium-high heat. Stir in the partially cooked veggies and beef, then simmer over medium-low heat until vegetables are tender, 5 to 10 minutes.

3 Add spinach and cook until wilted. Season with salt and pepper before serving.

* We used 1 pkg. classic mixed vegetables and 1 pkg. celery/onion/bell pepper blend.

Ramen & Beef Skillet

- ✔ 1 lb. lean ground beef
- ✔ 1 (3 oz.) pkg. chicken & mushroom flavored ramen noodles
- ✔ 2 (3 oz.) pkgs. chicken flavored ramen noodles
- ✔ 2 C. water
- ✔ 1 (14 oz.) pkg. frozen stir-fry vegetables

1 In a large skillet over medium heat, cook the beef until no longer pink, crumbling it with a wooden spoon as it cooks. Drain off the grease.

2 Add the three seasoning packets from the ramen noodles to the cooked beef in skillet. Cook and stir for 2 minutes and then transfer the meat to a bowl.

3 Add water to skillet and bring to a boil. Break noodles into chunks and add to skillet along with the vegetables. Return to a boil. Reduce heat to medium-low, cover skillet, and boil gently 3 to 5 minutes or until noodles are tender, stirring occasionally.

4 Stir in the meat and cook until heated through.

Bacon & Egg Brunch Roll-Up

- ✔ 8 bacon strips
- ✔ 1 C. egg substitute (such as Egg Beaters) or 4 eggs, beaten
- ✔ ⅛ tsp. black pepper
- ✔ ¼ tsp. dry mustard
- ✔ 1 (8 oz.) roll seamless crescent dough sheet
- ✔ ¾ C. shredded Colby Jack, Pepper Jack, or sharp cheddar cheese, divided

1 Preheat the oven to 375°. Cook the bacon in a big nonstick skillet over medium heat until browned and crisp; drain on paper towels. When cool, crumble the bacon. Discard the grease and lightly wipe out the skillet.

2 Pour the egg substitute into the same skillet over medium heat; cook and stir until set. Chop into bite-size pieces.

3 Line a rimmed baking sheet with parchment paper. Unroll the dough on the paper, pressing lightly to make an even rectangle about 12" long. Place the chopped eggs along the length of the dough, slightly off-center and stopping an inch from the ends. Top with most of the crumbled bacon and most of the cheese; reserve the remainder.

4 Fold one long side of dough over the filling, using the parchment paper to lift it up as needed. Fold the remaining long side over the filling and overlap dough at the top to make a log; pinch long seam and both ends together to seal well. Carefully roll the log over so seam is on the bottom.

5 Sprinkle the reserved bacon and cheese over the top of the roll, pressing gently so it stays in place. Bake 15 to 18 minutes or until crust is deep golden brown. Remove from the oven and let stand 5 minutes. Use a serrated knife to cut slices.

Steak with Saucy Mushrooms
AND *Pesto Cheese Bread*

- ✔ 1 (8 oz.) pkg. fresh mushrooms
- ✔ 4 T. butter, divided
- ✔ 4 tender boneless steaks (like sirloin or ribeye)
- ✔ ½ C. heavy cream
- ✔ Sea salt and black pepper to taste

1 Wash the mushrooms with cool water; slice and set aside.

2 Melt 2 tablespoons butter and brush it over both sides of steaks. Heat a large skillet over medium-high heat and add the steaks. Cook on one side for 3 to 5 minutes *(thicker steaks need more time than thin ones)*. Flip and cook to desired doneness *(3 to 5 minutes more for medium rare, approximately 145°)*. Transfer steaks to a plate and cover with foil to rest.

3 Carefully wipe out the skillet. Place skillet over medium heat and melt remaining 2 tablespoons butter. Stir in the mushrooms and cook until golden brown and softened. Stir in cream and simmer on medium-low heat until thickened. Season the mushrooms with sea salt and pepper, and serve over the steaks.

PESTO CHEESE BREAD
P. 60

Baked Pizza Burgers

- ✔ 3 T. pizza sauce, plus more for serving
- ✔ ⅓ C. Italian seasoned bread crumbs, divided
- ✔ 1 lb. lean ground beef
- ✔ ½ C. shredded Italian cheese blend or mozzarella cheese
- ✔ 4 hamburger buns
- ✔ Optional toppings (spinach or lettuce leaves, sliced tomato, and/or onion)

1 Preheat the oven to 350°. Cover the bottom of a 9 x 13" baking pan with parchment paper.

2 In a large bowl, combine 3 tablespoons pizza sauce and 2 tablespoons bread crumbs. Crumble the beef into the bowl and mix well with your hands.

3 Shape the beef mixture into eight thin patties, about 3½" in diameter. Place about 2 tablespoons cheese on four of the patties. Top each with a remaining patty and press them together to seal the edges and hold the cheese inside.

4 Pour the remaining bread crumbs onto a plate and coat both sides and edges of each stuffed patty in crumbs. Set them in the lined pan and bake for 10 minutes; flip and bake 10 to 13 minutes more or until juices run clear. Serve on buns with more pizza sauce, plus spinach, tomato, and onion as desired.

Toast those buns!

To toast burger buns, generously spritz the cut side of each bun half with cooking spray and place them sprayed side down in a skillet over medium-high heat; cook until golden brown and toasty.

Sour Cream Potatoes

Spray a 4- to 6-quart slow cooker with cooking spray. In a bowl, mix 1 (10.75 oz.) can cream of mushroom with roasted garlic soup, 1 C. sour cream, and 1½ C. shredded Colby Jack cheese. Pour half of a 32 oz. package frozen cubed hash browns into the slow cooker. Top with half the sour cream mixture and remaining hash browns. Spread remaining sour cream mixture over the potatoes. Cover and cook on HIGH for 3 to 4 hours. Before serving, sprinkle with paprika, salt, black pepper, and chopped chives if you'd like. *Serves 8*

Pesto Cheese Bread

Cut a loaf of Vienna bread into ¾" slices *(don't cut through the bottom)*. Set the loaf on a large piece of foil. Mix 6 T. melted butter and 3 T. sun-dried tomato pesto. Brush some of the mixture between each bread slice and brush remainder over the top. Cut 8 deli-style slices of provolone cheese into smaller pieces and place them between the bread slices. Crimp the foil closely around the bottom half of loaf and set packet on the center oven rack. Bake at 375° for 15 minutes or until the top is golden brown and cheese is melted. Serve warm. *Makes 12 to 15 slices*